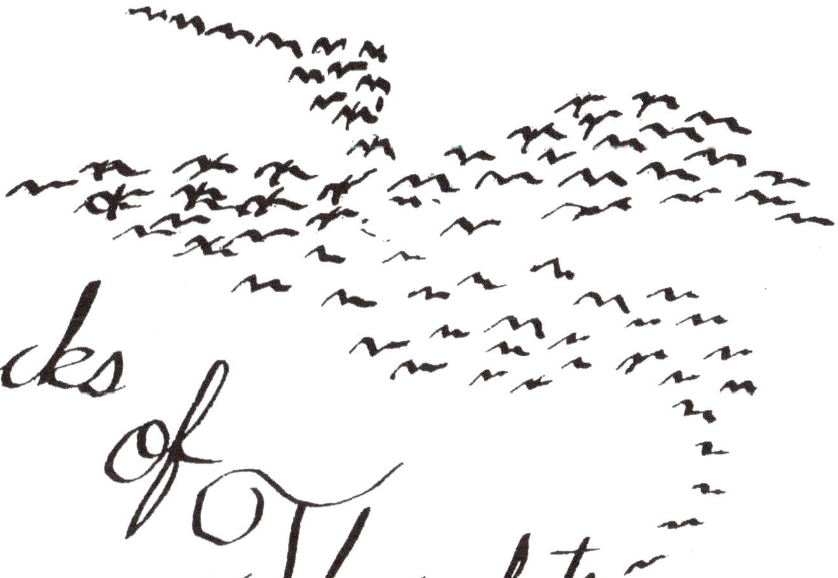

Flocks of Thoughts

By Janette Bach

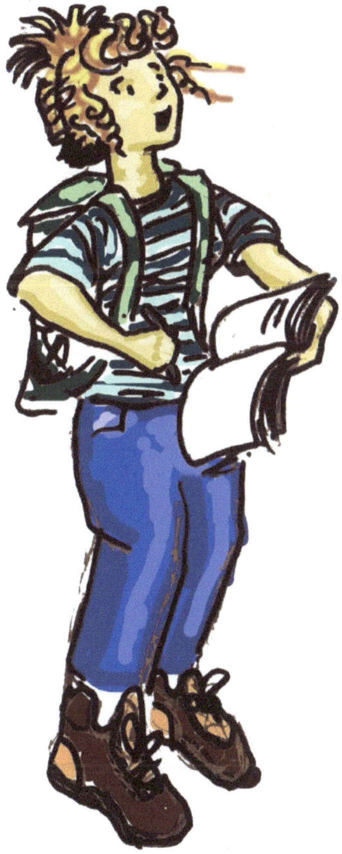

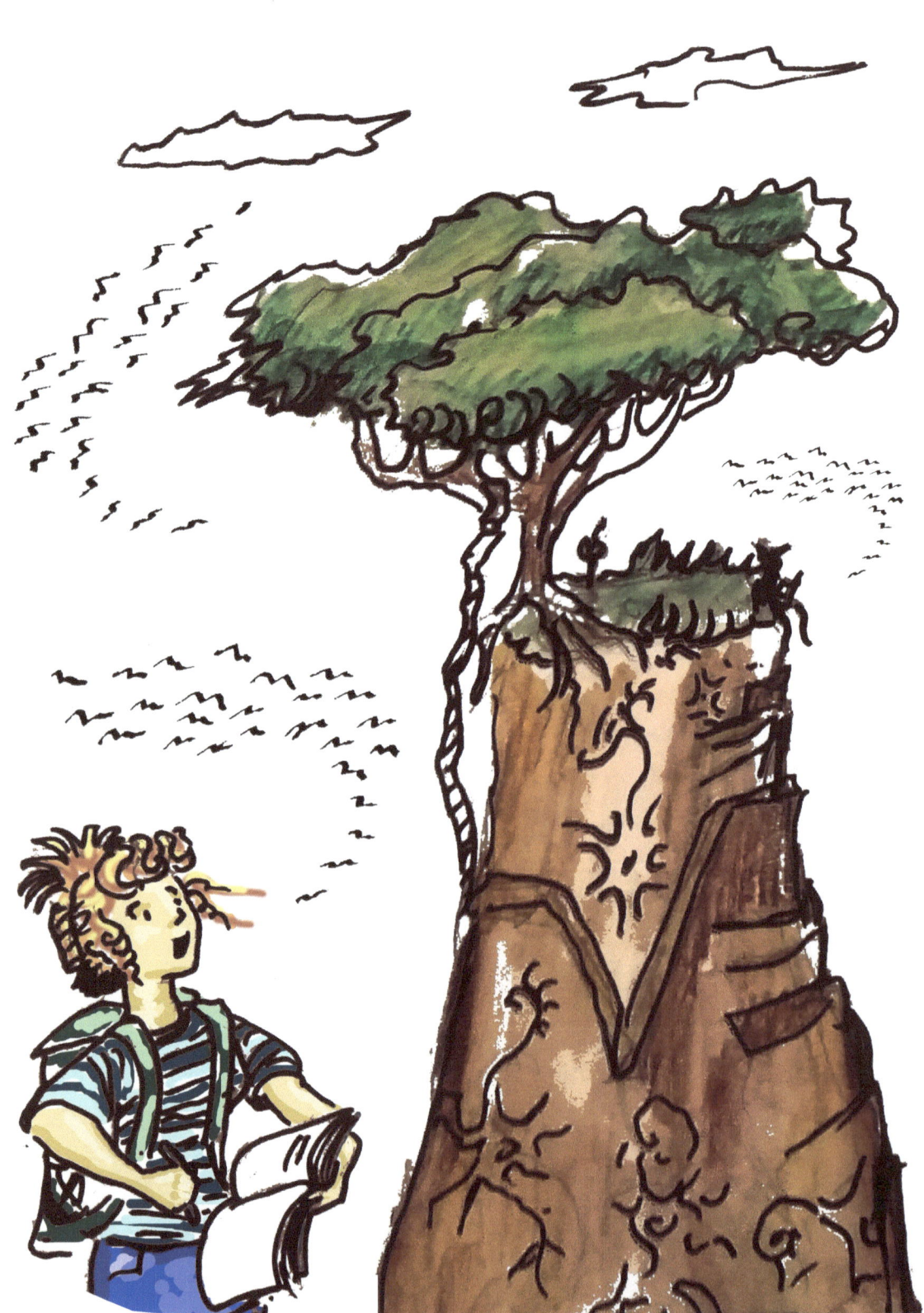

I have been to Zion and Yellowstone. I have stood in wonder at the cliffs of the Grand Canyon. Yosemite's marvels are not lost on me. But this journal is not about those trips. This is field sketchbook from a hike that floored me. I was on an adventure into the collective unconscious of the human mind.

How did I get there? That my friend is a complicated story. But right now, I want to talk about the birds. The creatures of wings that populate our minds when certain thoughts come into play.

These birds look different yet familiar. I have done what I could to recreate their likenesses here in this journal. No camera could capture them. As I drew furiously, I tried record the types of thoughts they like to occupy.

So this is my first study in the flocks of the mind.

Athene Trek

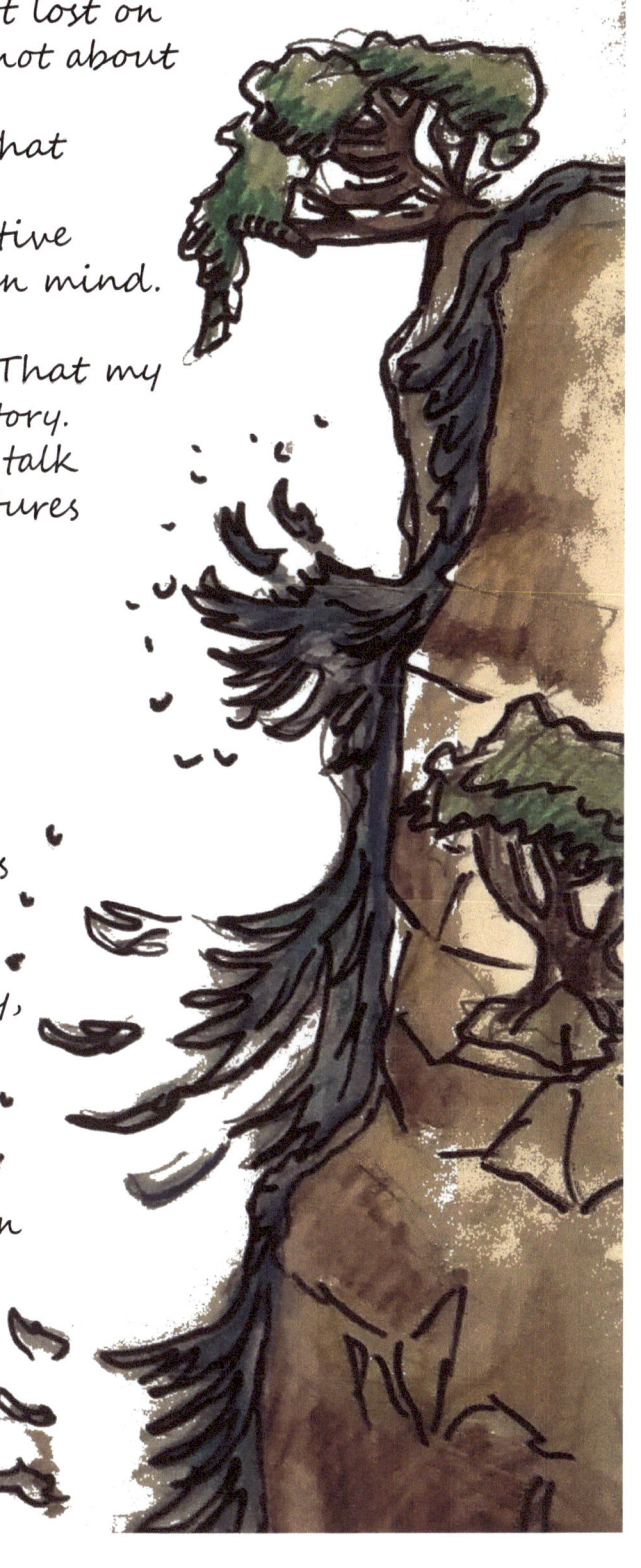

The Striped Rush

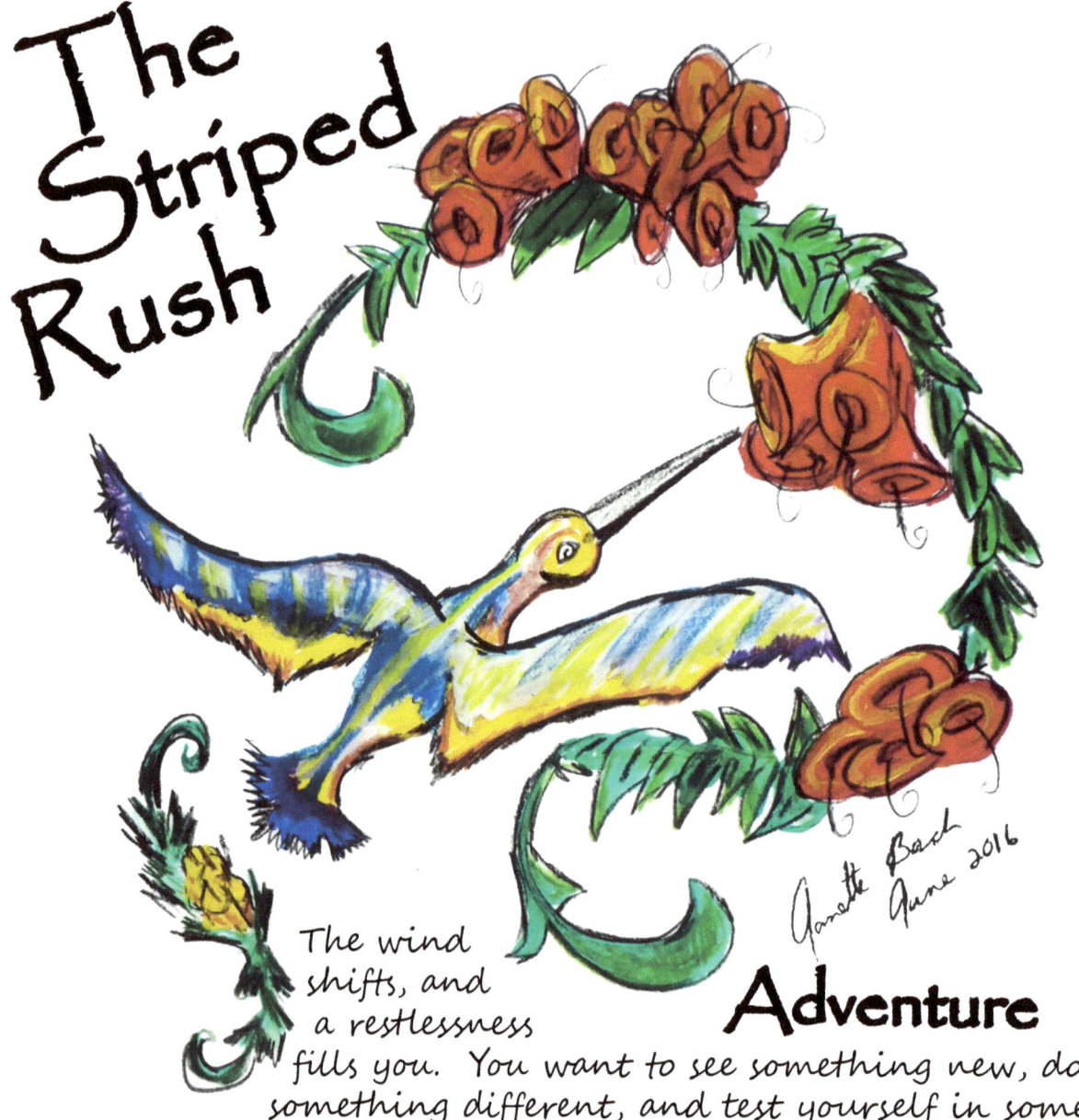

Janette Bach
June 2016

Adventure

The wind shifts, and a restlessness fills you. You want to see something new, do something different, and test yourself in some way. Your thoughts spin and images collide. You think of rafting, climbing, snorkeling, and hiking.

As you swear you smell the breeze from some exotic locale, you hear the rushing climbing song of the Striped Rush. This bird's bright yellow colors sparkle iridescent new ideas in your mind, and the blue stripes lead you through the order of arranging a trip. Their bleeding, imperfect lines reminding you **nothing goes according to plan. But isn't that what adventure is about?**

You have just filed your tenth report or done this chore for the hundredth time. You pause and you wonder: Is this all it's about? Why am I here? Why am I doing this? Does this matter? You sigh and remember all the people in your life counting on you. The people who need those reports.

This shy little bird hums, not a whistle or chirp just a hum. Seems like an unimportant noise, but this hum reaches your bones. It reflects the hum of the world around you, but you realize it is unique to you. You find yourself humming along. You are one with the world, but something unique. Life is what you make it. The Pink Widget: its pink feathers remind you of your unique mind. The yellow highlights remind you that you need to orchestrate these mundane tasks into fun. **You can do it!**

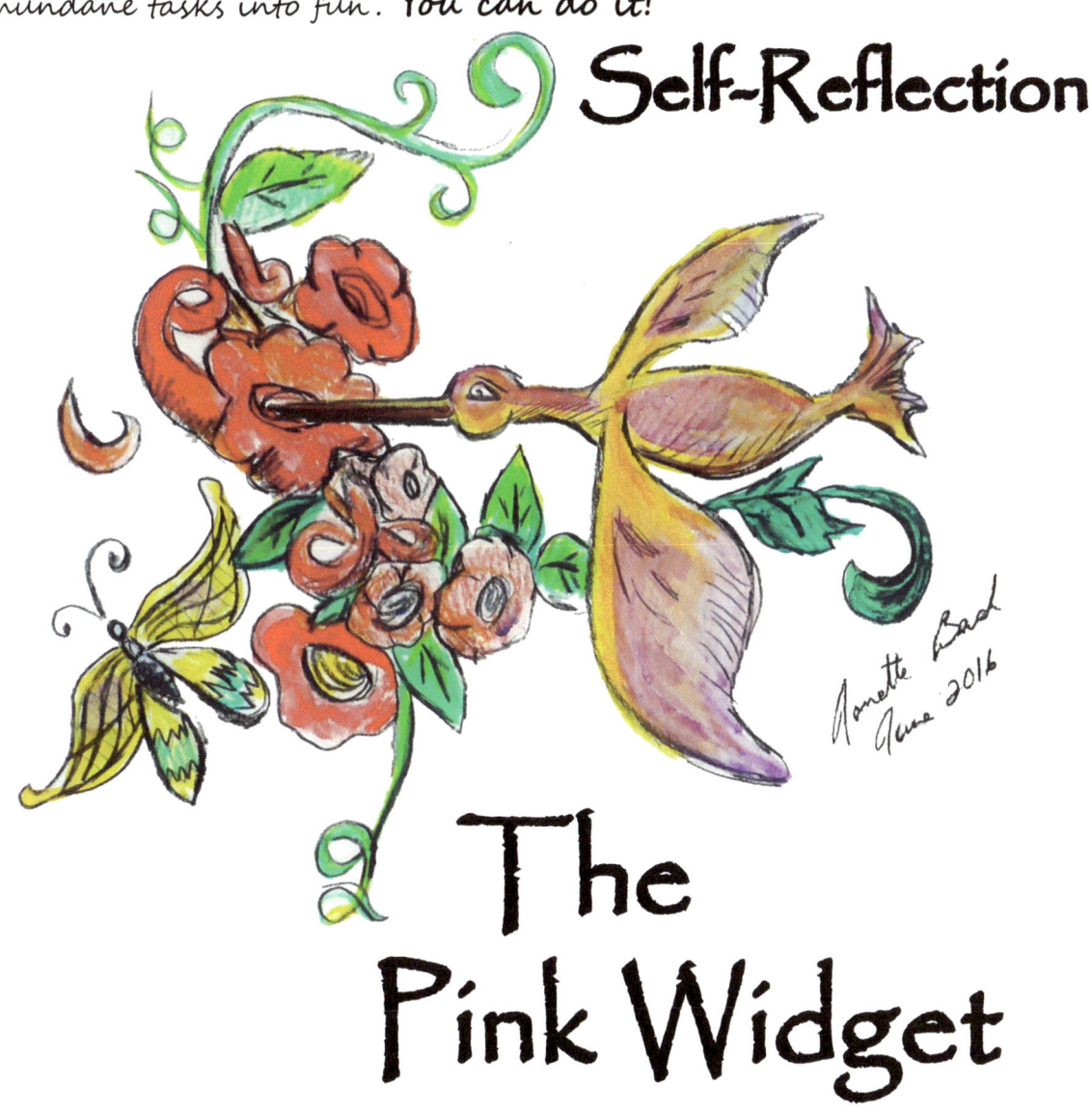

Self-Reflection

The Pink Widget

The Blue Thrush

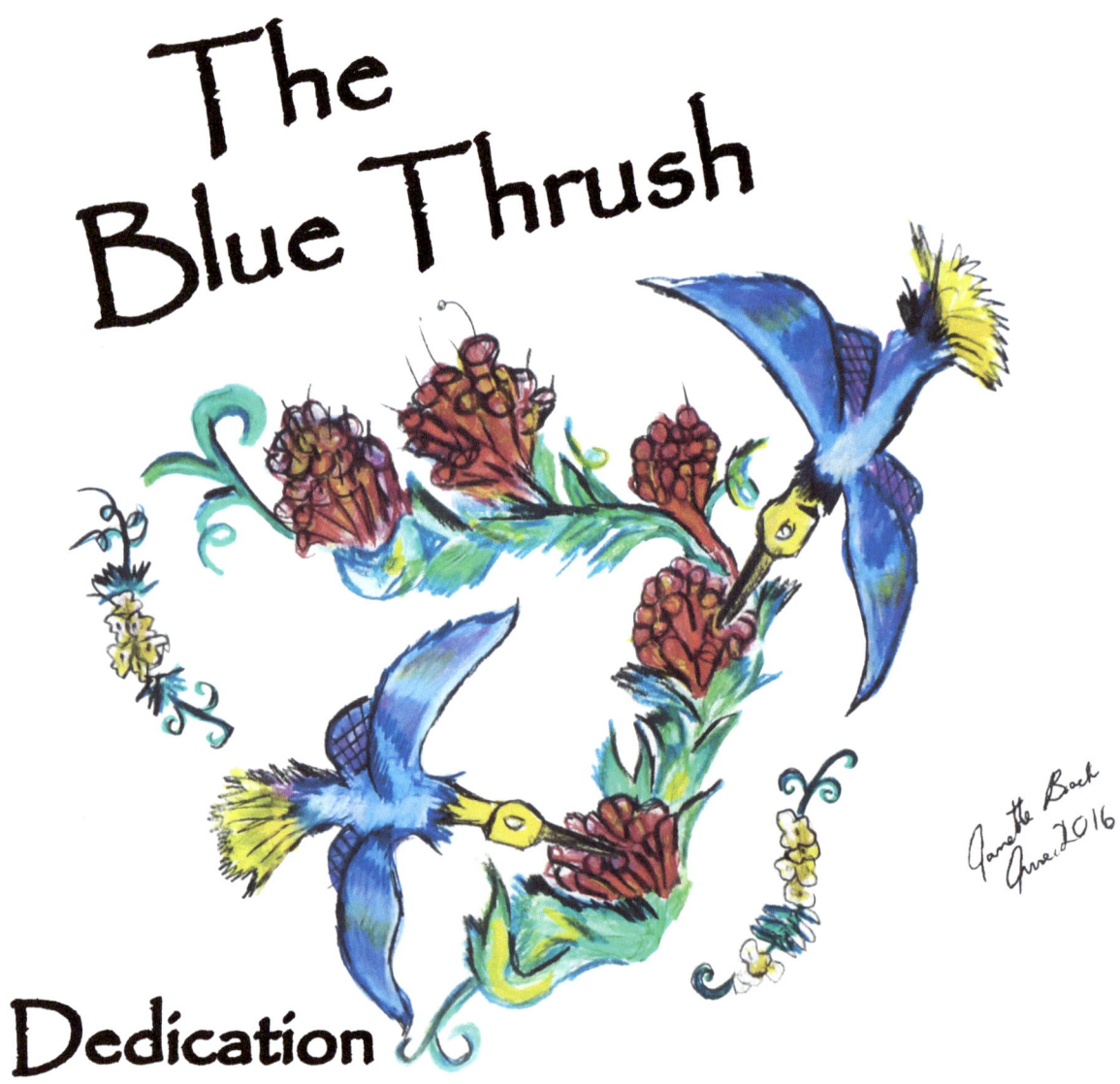

Dedication

That chubby hand grasps your finger tight. The windows rattle, & you are reminded how rough the world outside is. You pull your baby close; you hold on tight. You promise to be there, to always be there. No matter how hard, no matter what comes your way. This was just a concept before, an idea you wanted to have in yourself, but now you know.

You will give your life, your mind, and your body to raise this child. To nurture them & help them grow. These birds come in fierce & strong. Their song is a steady beat - a hammering drum.   They come in singularly. Then swarm. Their blue feathers remind you of the unyielding strength of the crashing ocean, the endlessness of the sky, and the depths of the universe. They are the Blue Thrush. There is no turning back! Their song is strong & **you are resolved in your decision!**

The board beneath your fingers shatters. The wood you have been carving, and had just the way you wanted, couldn't take it anymore. It dissolves before you. Splinters fall away and puncture your fingers, and you stare at the remains. Weeks of work reduced to this pile of wood. You take a moment, stare at the chisel in your hand, and remember the grain of the wood.

You look at your pile of wood. You look for what is different, what you think will endure, what you want to do. You select another piece, and that is when they come: their song a steady, slowly climbing hum. Their music hits before they fly past your mind's eye.

The Patterned Swarmer birds flutter like butterflies, their wings patterned with geometric shapes. They dance among your ideas and rearrange them. In fluttering motions moving and setting. Moving and setting till you realize that was the path you wanted.
You can do this, and it will be even better this time!

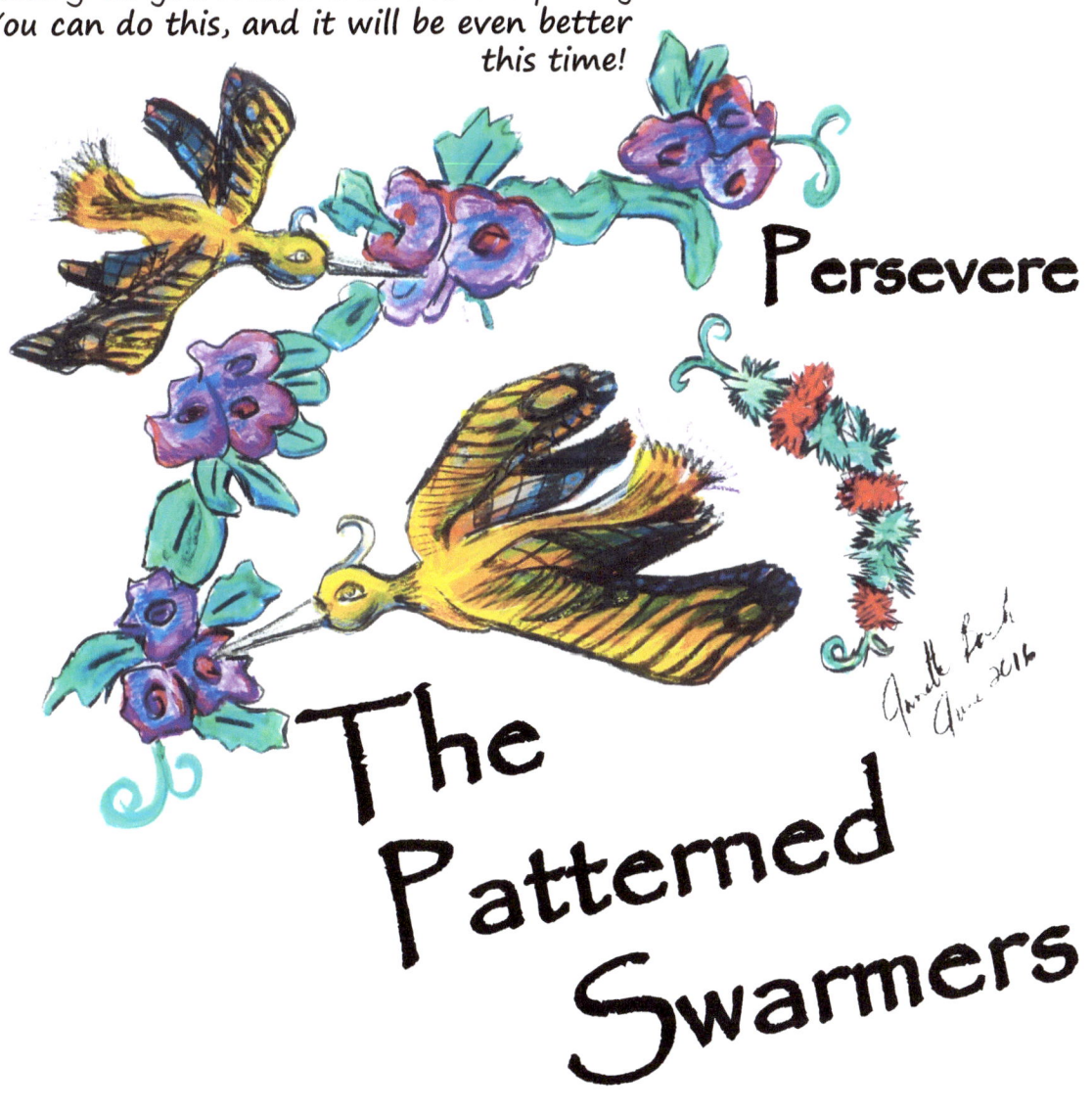

Persevere

The Patterned Swarmers

Veined Fire

Joy

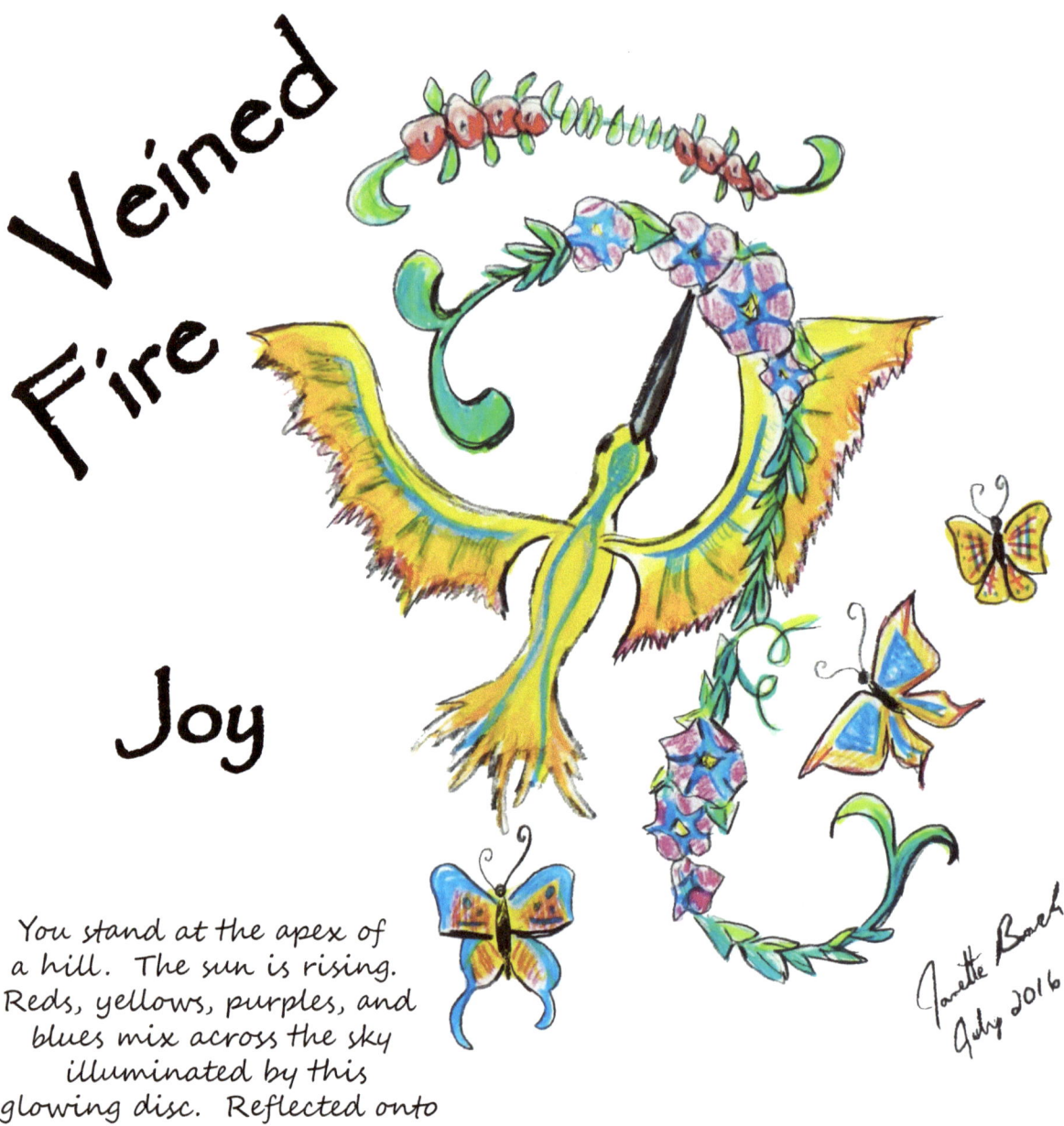

You stand at the apex of a hill. The sun is rising. Reds, yellows, purples, and blues mix across the sky illuminated by this glowing disc. Reflected onto the popcorn clouds surrounding you. It had been a trek in the semi darkness to get to this point to catch this moment. You stumbled on roots, rocks, and uneven terrain. But you made it. You are here. You get to witness this: the day beginning again!

The Veined Fire birdsong is bright and luminous. Haunting and soothing at the same time. It vibrates through you, and you feel like it makes you glow. The bright yellow feathers seem to be made of liquid sunshine. The blue feathers out structures that allow these moments to happen and be perceived. **Life is good and you are alive!**

You start in one room. You pull the broom down and sweep. You come to a threshold and you venture further. In the beginning, doing the whole house had been daunting, and now you look down the hall, and you realize it's not that bad. You tackle the hall and then another room.

Diligent Damsels sing jazzy sounds that complement each other.   Their electric colors of yellow and blue highlight their purple variegated plumage. The yellow and purple contrast – full of energy and the blue giving your thoughts a place to rest. They swoop and glide, leaking energy like batteries. Spurring you forward. **You can do this!**

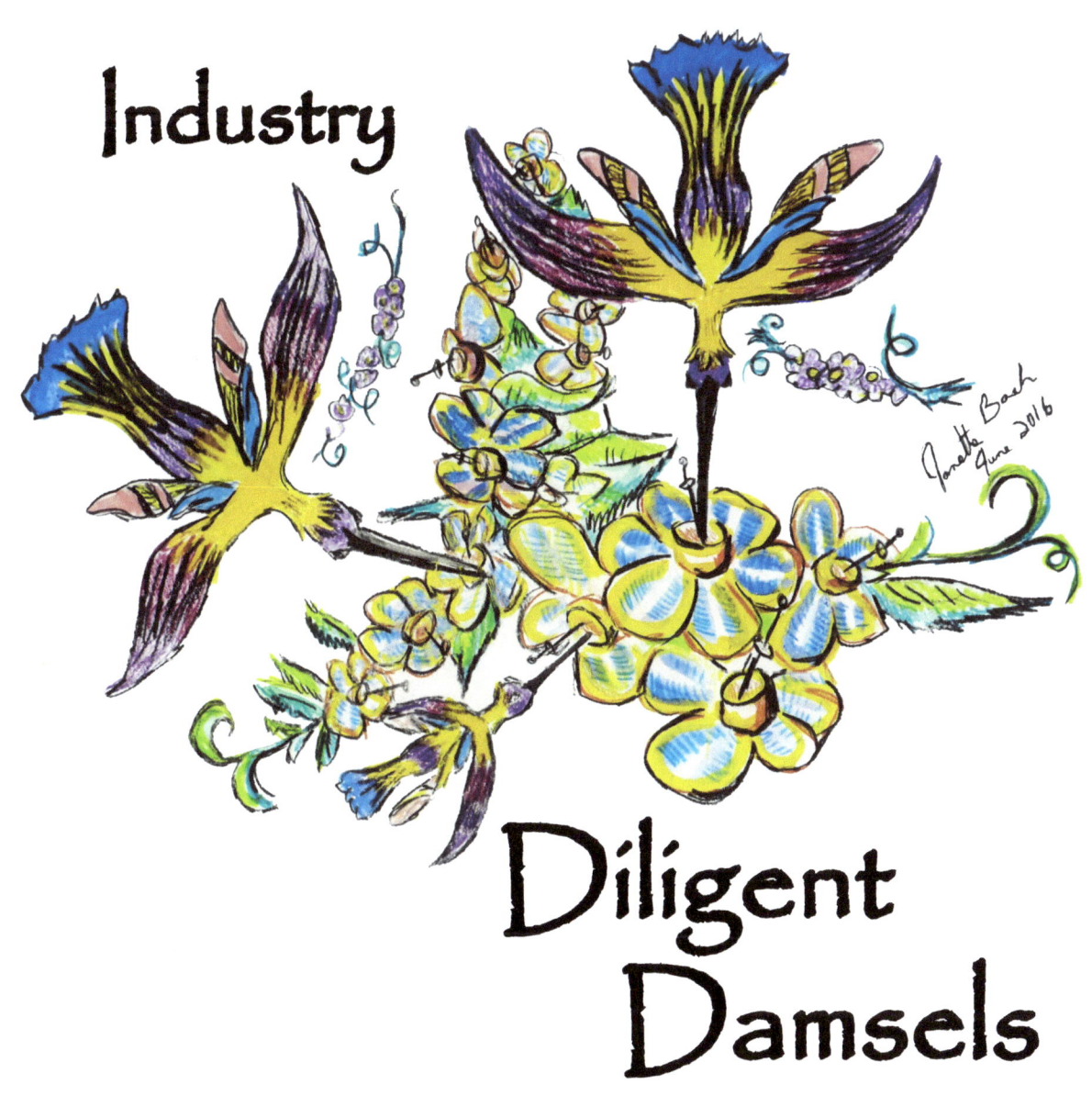

Industry

Diligent
Damsels

Your hands are full, and you are trying to take a ton of packages to a shipping facility. You reach the door, but can't find a way to juggle the packages to open the door. You pause in front of the door. A person you have never seen before and may never see again sees you, opens the door, and holds it for you. You give them a grateful smile and stammer a thank you. This reminds you how beautiful the dance of culture can be.

Fluted shrills and long lazy flights. The patterns of their flight remind you of swirling patterns. Their orange, green blue patterns highlight their structure in flight. They themselves look like flowers. It's the Daffodil Comet.

You cannot help but appreciate their beauty: a reminder that **there is beauty everywhere!**

Daffodil Comet

Beauty

Janette Boal
June 2016

Tranversal Sparrow　　Spiritual

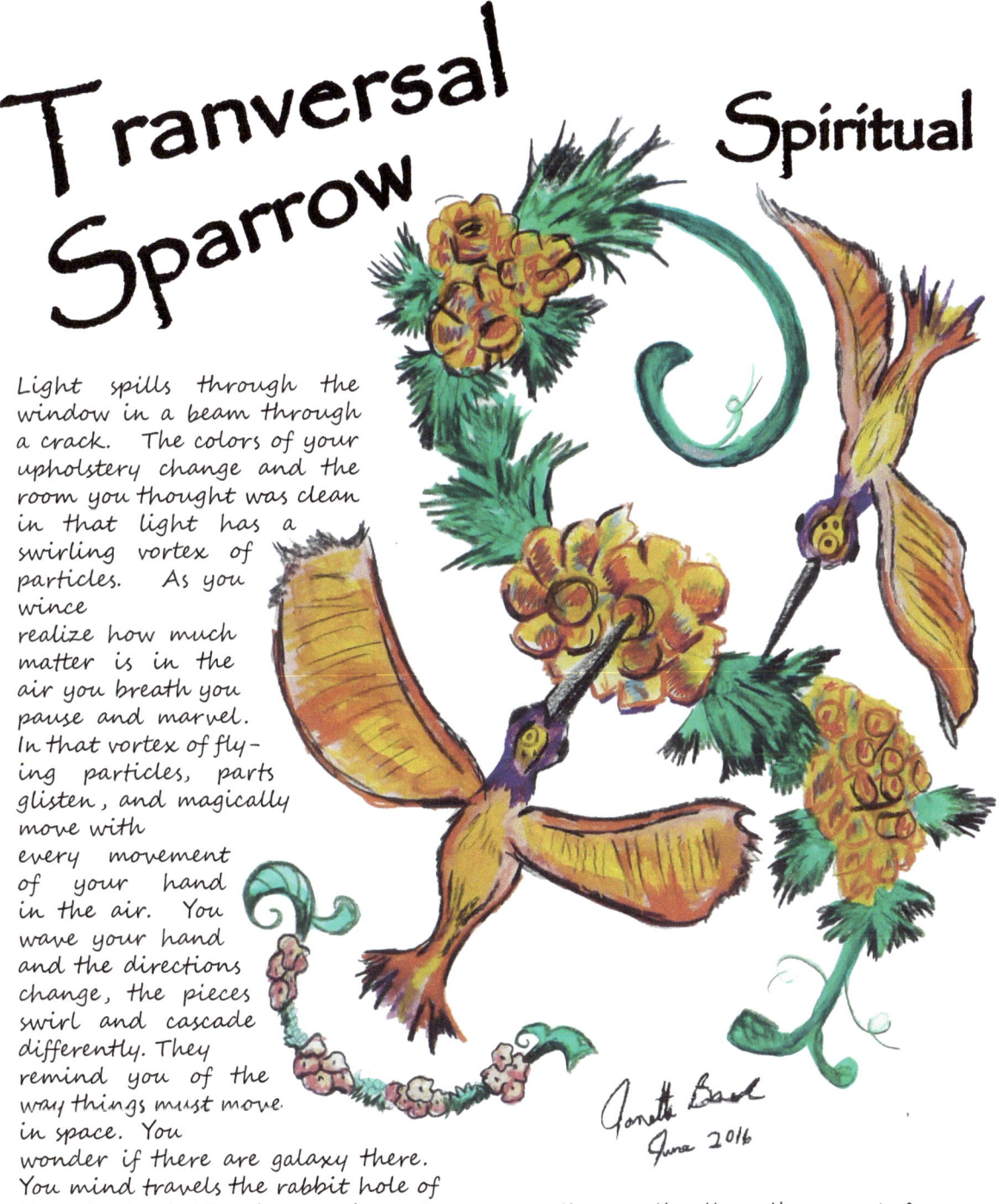

Light spills through the window in a beam through a crack. The colors of your upholstery change and the room you thought was clean in that light has a swirling vortex of particles. As you wince realize how much matter is in the air you breath you pause and marvel. In that vortex of fly-ing particles, parts glisten, and magically move with every movement of your hand in the air. You wave your hand and the directions change, the pieces swirl and cascade differently. They remind you of the way things must move in space. You wonder if there are galaxy there. You mind travels the rabbit hole of thought to civilizations and creatures on matter smaller than the specs before you.

Their song is haunting and atmospheric. Seems to be coming from everywhere and nowhere at once. The plumage on their heads have the circles within circles, reminding you of the thoughts with in thoughts and the wholeness of the universe. Yellow bright, and tinged in red, ruddy clouds the Transversal Sparrow drip complex thoughts. The purple headdress reminding you that there is always more to perceive and consider. **Thank the universe for that!**

Life has gotten so complex; you stare at the tax forms. Item three baffles you and you're not sure if you have all your receipts. The news is blowing up with complex issues that you wonder if there was anything you can do to help. A longing fills you. You long for a time when your biggest worry was what game to play next, and whether there will be Brussel sprouts at dinner.

The Rainbow Cruisers' song is simple and playful. You find yourself thinking of climbing trees and nursery rhymes. Their rainbow colors are iridescent, and they seem to strobe through each other as they fly in playful groups in your mind. They begin with a simple game of tag, and then the game evolves from there. You start to notice that even though play seems simple, it gets complex fast, and the game evolves. **And what you're staring at is just another complex game and you can figure out these rules too!**

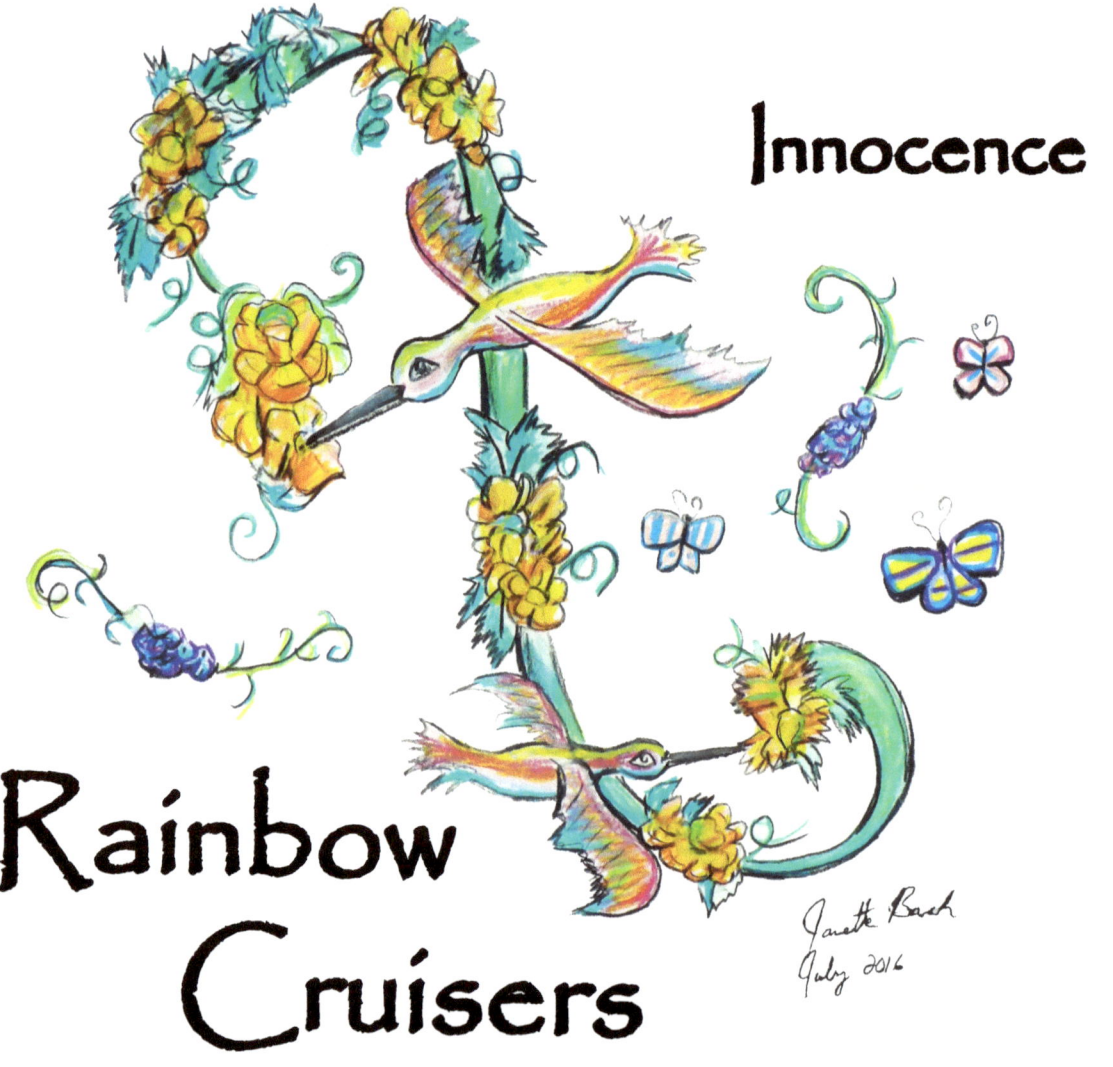

Innocence

Rainbow Cruisers

Fire Throng

Hope

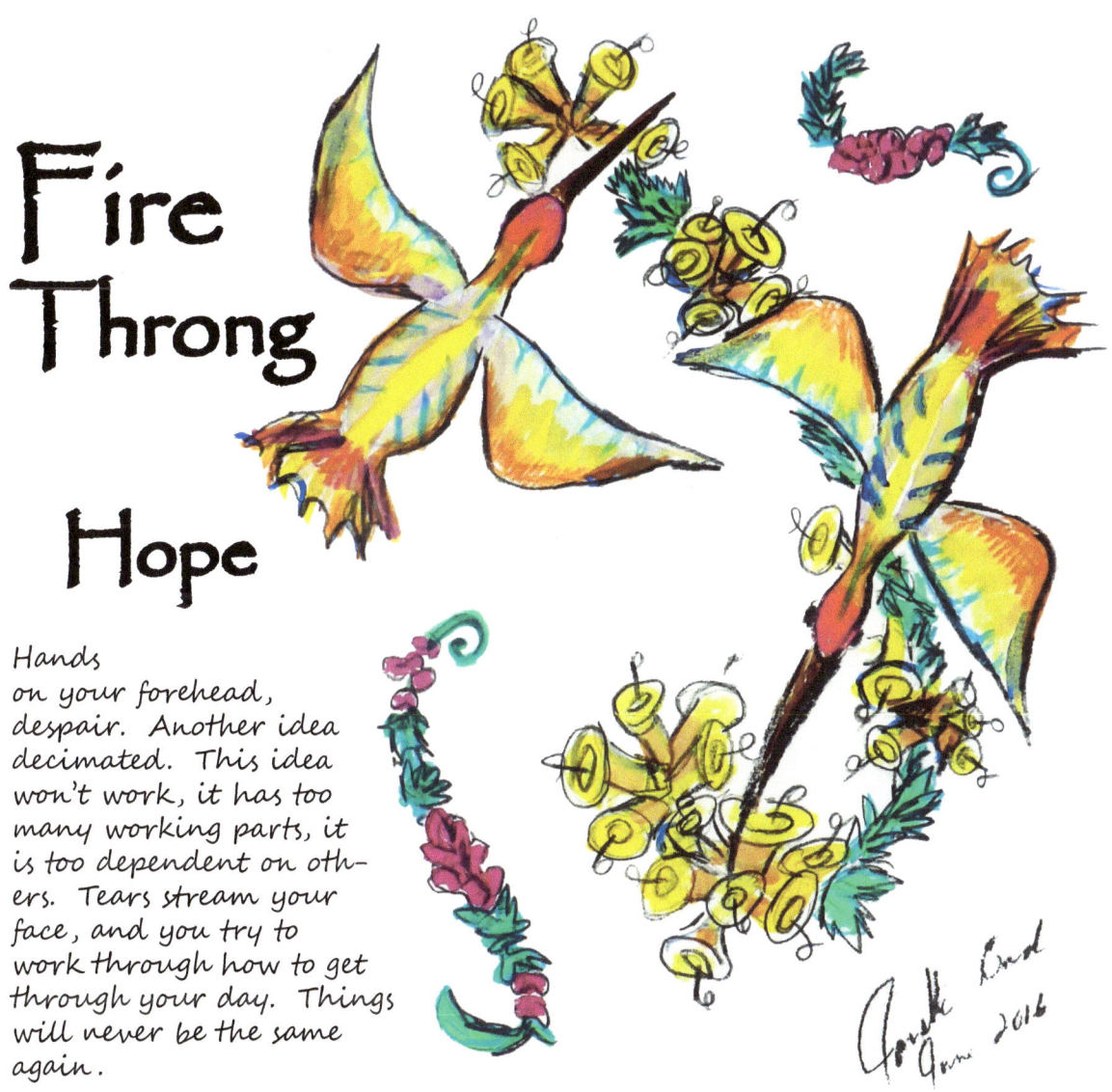

Hands
on your forehead,
despair. Another idea
decimated. This idea
won't work, it has too
many working parts, it
is too dependent on oth-
ers. Tears stream your
face, and you try to
work through how to get
through your day. Things
will never be the same
again.

You mind is in this rendition of taps and this little melody begins. You protest, you're upset damn it, how dare anything cheerful and teasing come in. The melody of the Fire Throng is catchy, upbeat. It reminds of you of the wheel of time, the adaptability of the human body, and spirit. The sound has the rhythm of a clock and the beat of blood in the veins.

You blink in your mind, and it starts with one; then blink again, and then there is two. Eventually it's a swarm. Bright fire shadowed birds of light punctuating the darkness of the rambling idea. Their yellow and white plumage glow cleansing the debris. The emotions of the moment leave for seconds as you piece together what ideas they highlight, recombining them. **Not all is lost**. There is a chance! Think through it differently, come at it a different way!

You are going about your day. You are focused on what needs to be done. Out of nowhere, an attractive stranger gives you a smile and a compliment on how you make your clothes look amazing. You pause and take a moment to talk and thank them. You give them a compliment.

You start to talk about small things. You are definitely not identical, but your ideas support each other, and hold each other up. You both laugh and just want to keep talking. Everything feels great. Different, but interesting.

Their song starts like a crackling flame. It warms you and puts you on guard. The song then plays out like a jazz riff, different with no compass, but compelling and fun. It is the Flamed Warbler and it takes your breath away. **It is surprising what will go together and will complement one another.**

Complement

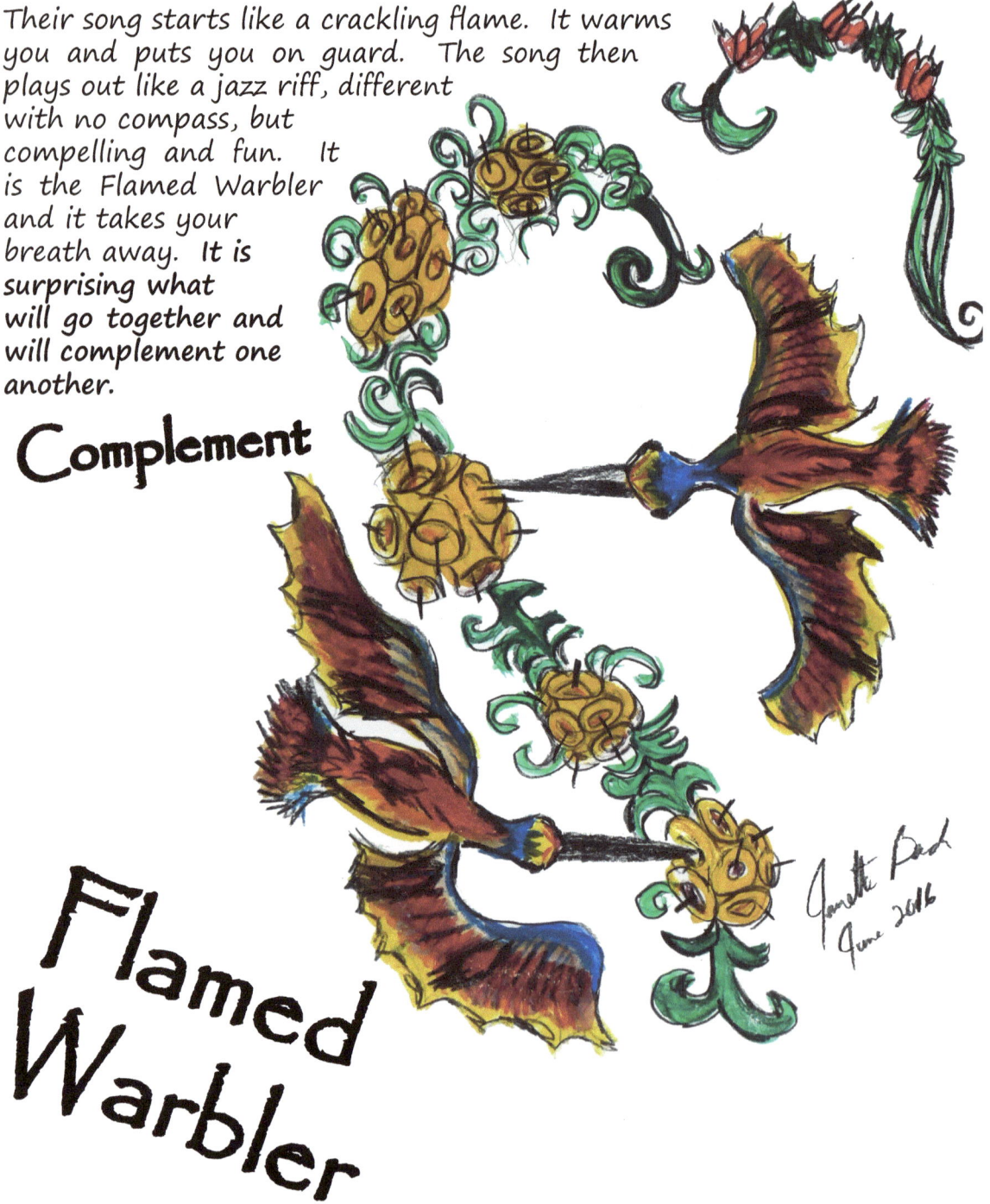

Flamed Warbler

Partnership

Pink Punch

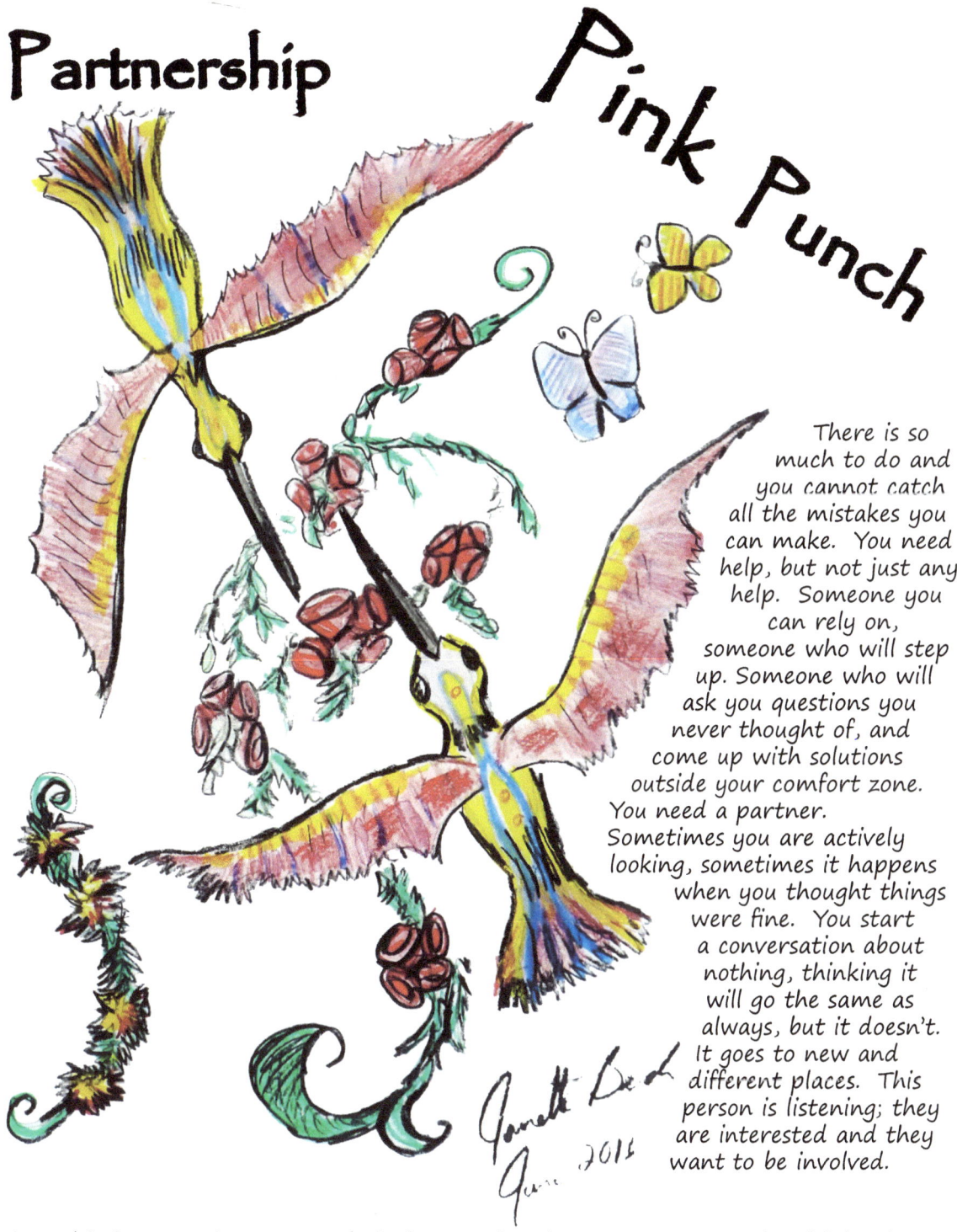

There is so much to do and you cannot catch all the mistakes you can make. You need help, but not just any help. Someone you can rely on, someone who will step up. Someone who will ask you questions you never thought of, and come up with solutions outside your comfort zone. You need a partner. Sometimes you are actively looking, sometimes it happens when you thought things were fine. You start a conversation about nothing, thinking it will go the same as always, but it doesn't. It goes to new and different places. This person is listening; they are interested and they want to be involved.

These birds come in twos and their song is a harmony. One going high, the other going low. They fly together yet stay individuals in their flight. The Pink Punch is always unexpected. Their colors at first seem incongruous. The pink garish and flashy against the yellow and blue of the tried and true. But it grows on you. You understand, no one person is the answer to everything. There is more to be and discover in a journey together. There will be compromises and wins, **but it will never be boring!**

Violet Striped Warbler

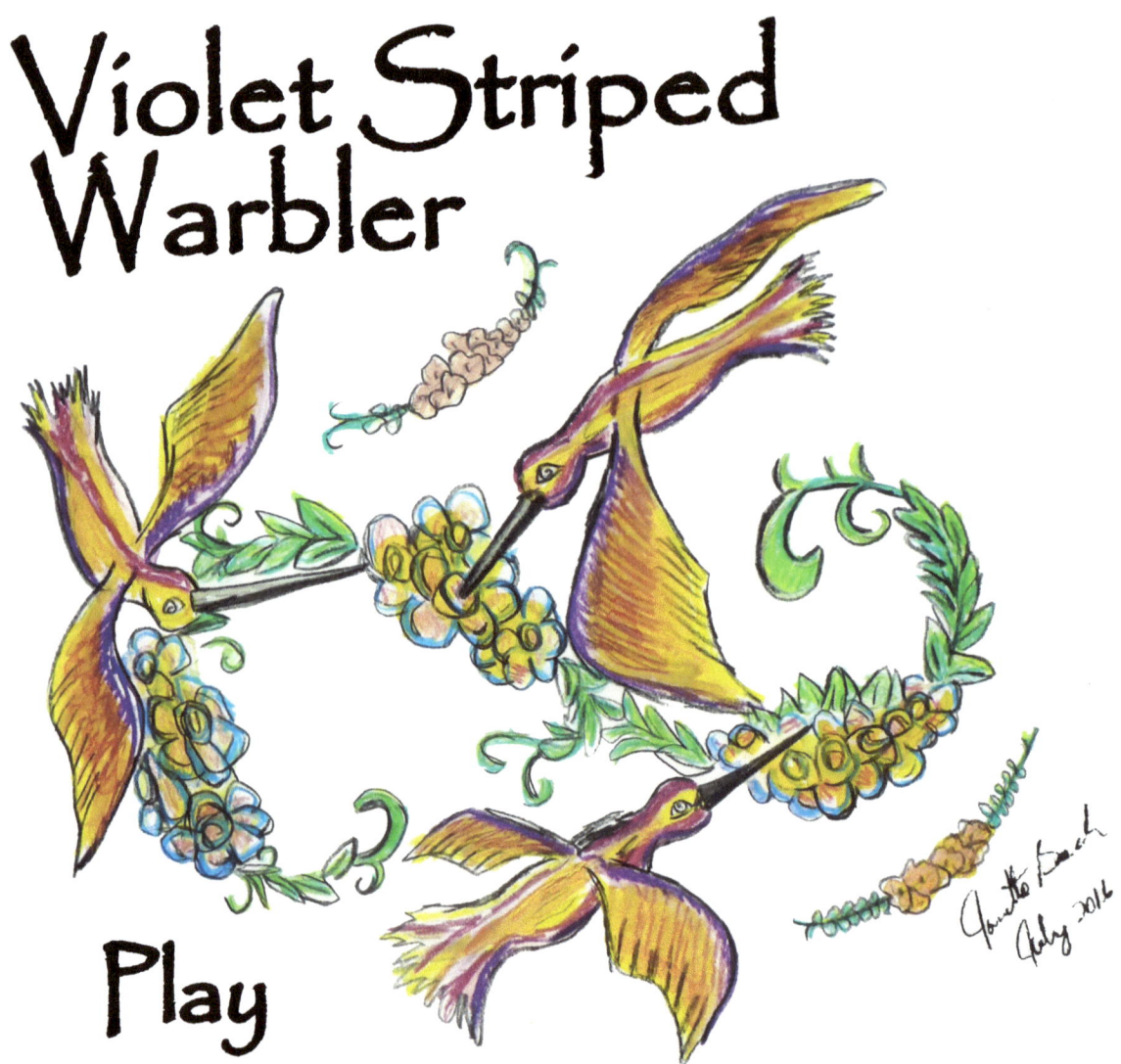

Play

You just finished a particularly long work week. The challenges were amazing and serious, but you met most of them, and put as much effort you could in the ones you couldn't finish. Your mind is fatigued. It needs to do something not so important. Something light, something that makes you laugh, and your heart sing. You think about downhill skiing or going to a movie. Something ouside the office and your own mind. You are ready to have fun.

As you turn your thoughts to lighter concerns, these birds sing a playful jig. They fly in your mind in a dance and spin into games. The Violet Striped Warblers' plumage streaks by in a purple striped blur. As they fly by all those fun things are reflected in the after images they leave in your mind. Their movements tickle and amuse. **You find yourself on the verge of telling a joke!**

You have been planning and scheming for a while now. You bought everything you need. It is time. Time to move thoughts into realities. You begin. You open your first package, then the next. The assembly begins.

The Bold Bludgeon doesn't pause, it flies straight in its song, a call to arms and you want to join it. Sure, you realize mistakes can be made, but you can't plan forever. It is time to move, time to do something. The magenta edging reminds you of the passion that sparked the idea to begin with. The yellow feathers blaze, and the line blue taunts you with the truth you learn from this endeavor. All action results in a knowledge of the blue line of truth!

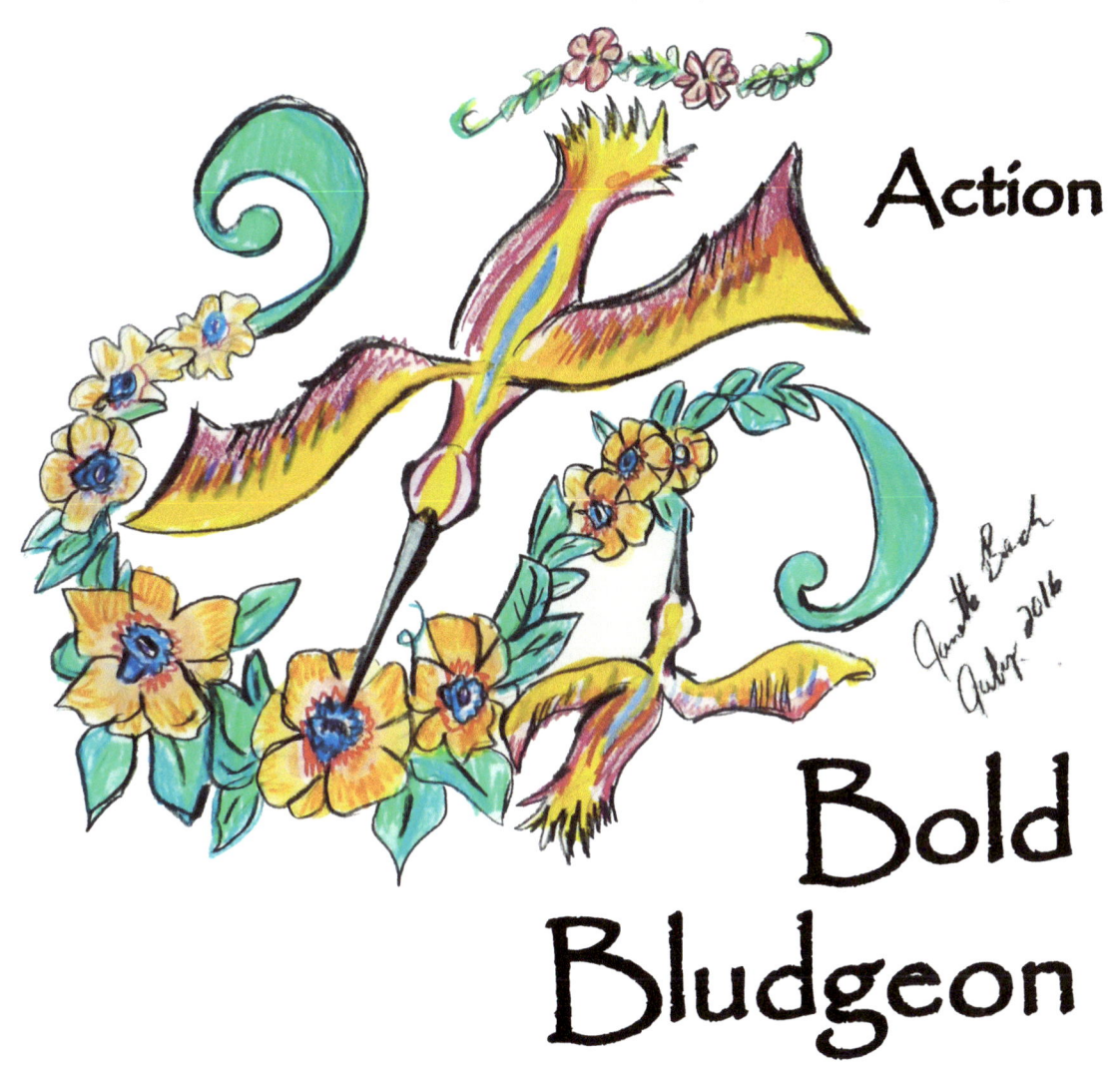

Action

Bold
Bludgeon

Meta Magpie

Order

As
your
mind
dumps a pile
of new ideas into
a yearning mass, you
crave something that will
make it all easier to find, to
grasp and comprehend. You bite your
lip and rub your forehead and start to
excavate this mass. You pull the layers away. You
categorize and find where it fits into what you know and what you
have never seen before.

This bird is a bird that flies with purpose and direction. It helps
with the snags, and hums. There is a patient quality to it. It takes
time to comb through and help dissect what you are looking at.
Because the one thing the Meta Magpie craves is understanding.
And to do that, things must be perceived entirely and dissected
toughly. **This takes time and patience.** Once understood, they fit
into the frame of your mind and become pathways for even new
ideas.

Janette Bach
June 2016

That is amazing, I got to do that! I feel alive when I try that! My senses open and everything in the world feels right! Could be writing, dancing, hiking, building, even computation. It is different for each person. You name a thing that any human has ever done and there is someone out there that has big opinions about how it is done, and how amazing it makes them feel.

When you find a passion, that is when these Phoenixes appear. Bright and blazing lighting up your senses and setting everything in your mind and body ablaze. Their song a Magnum Opus. You need to do this! You want to do this! **You can't wait to do it again!**

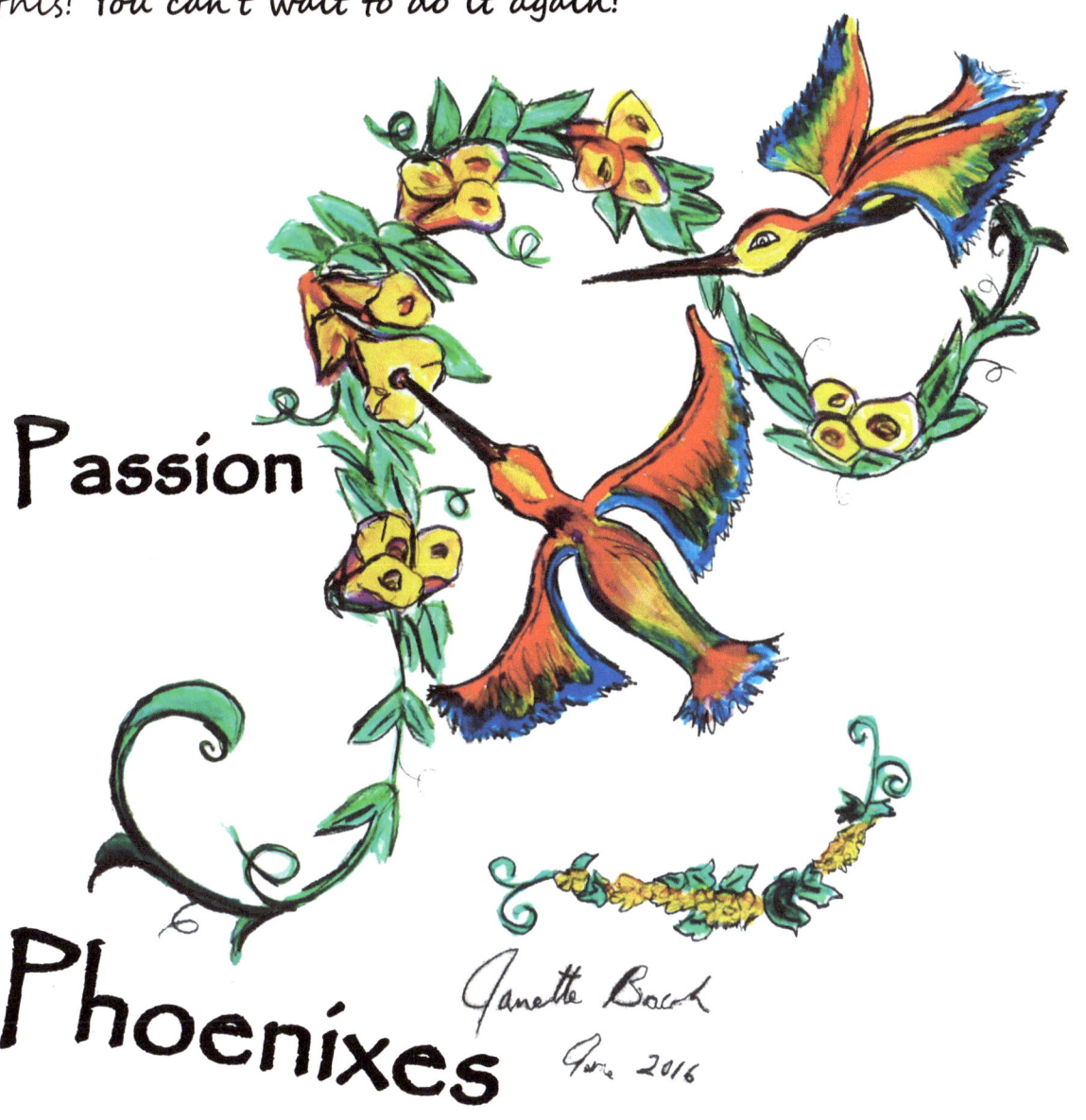

Passion

Phoenixes

Janette Bach
June 2016

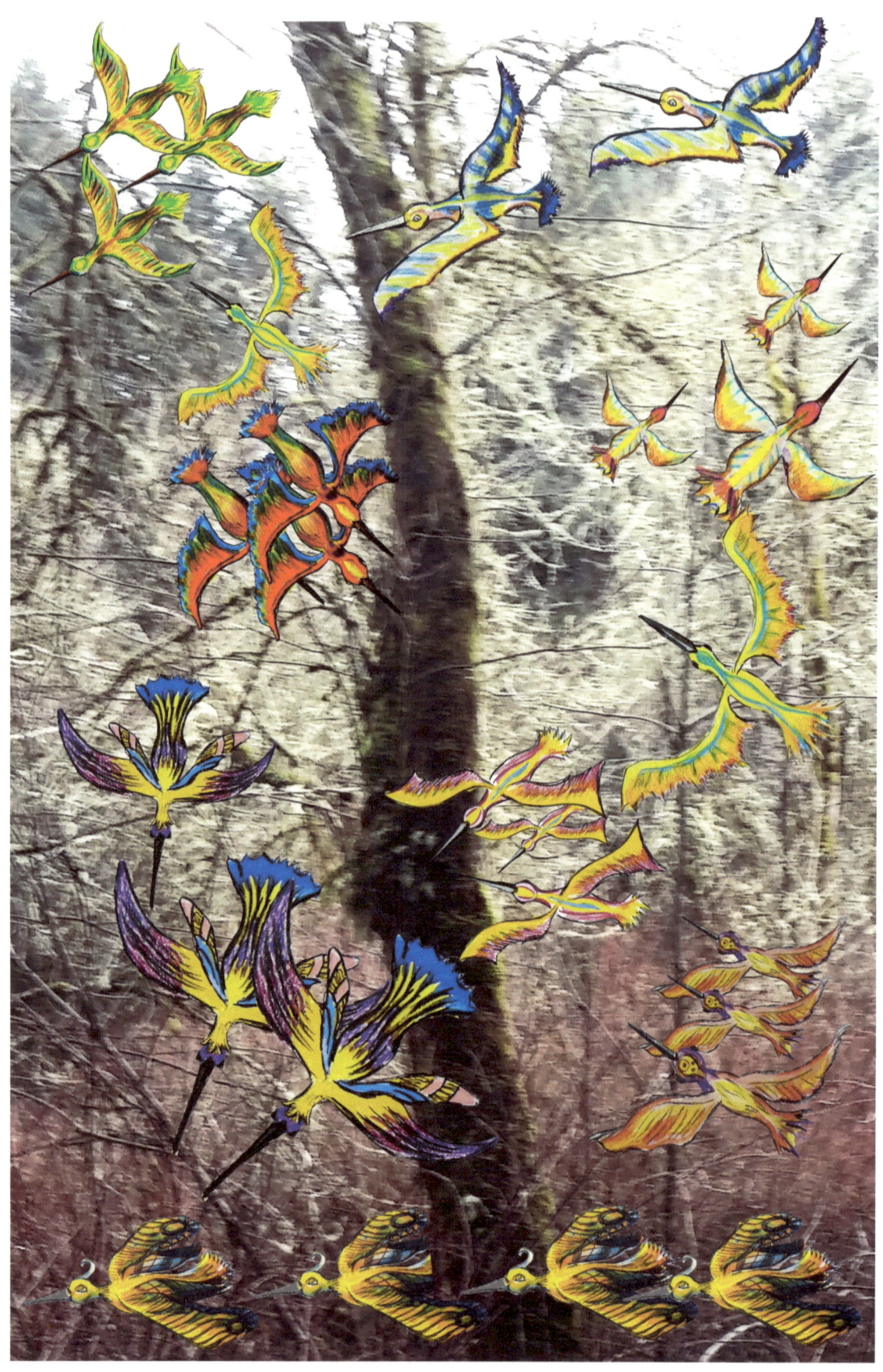

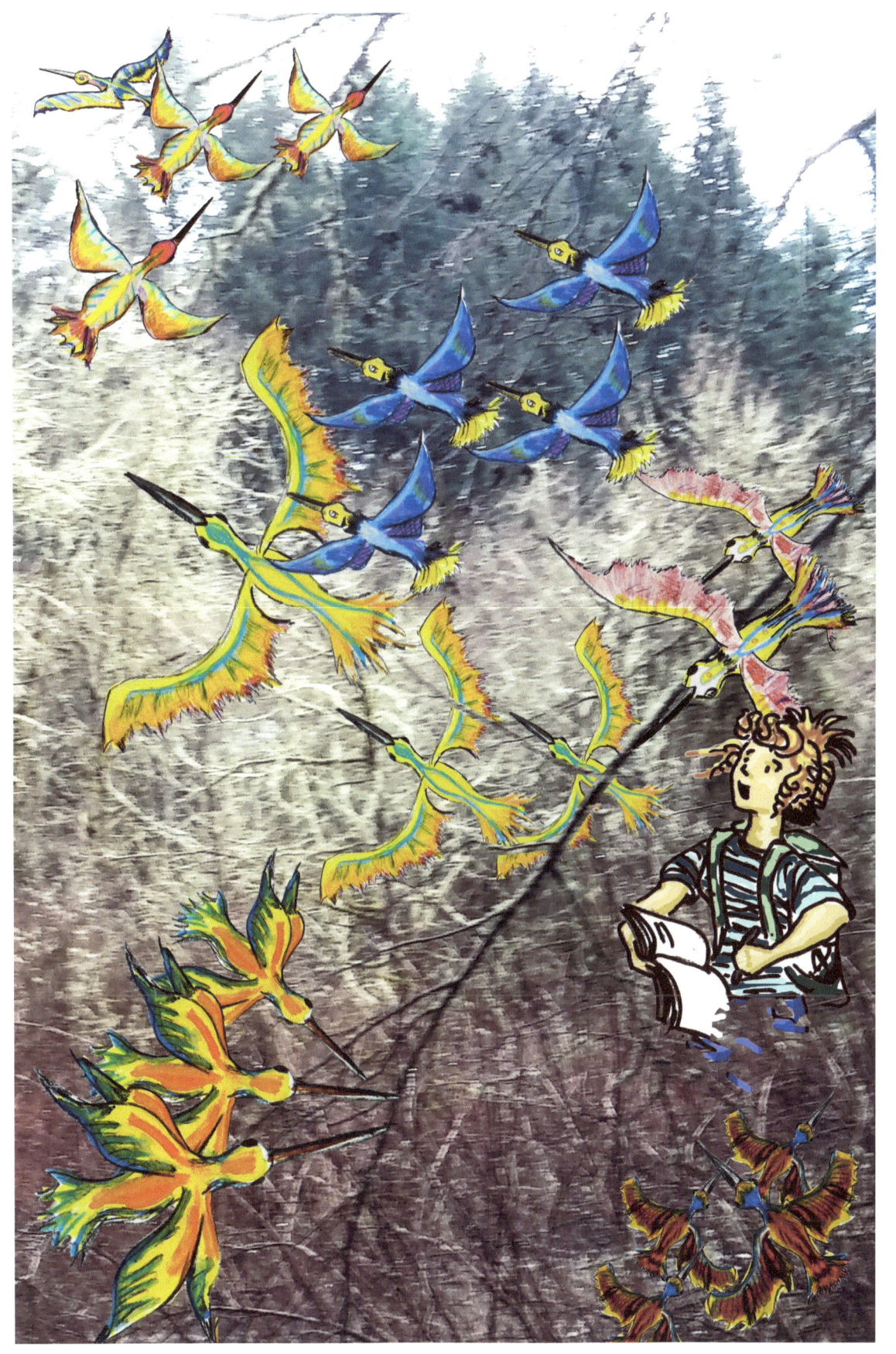

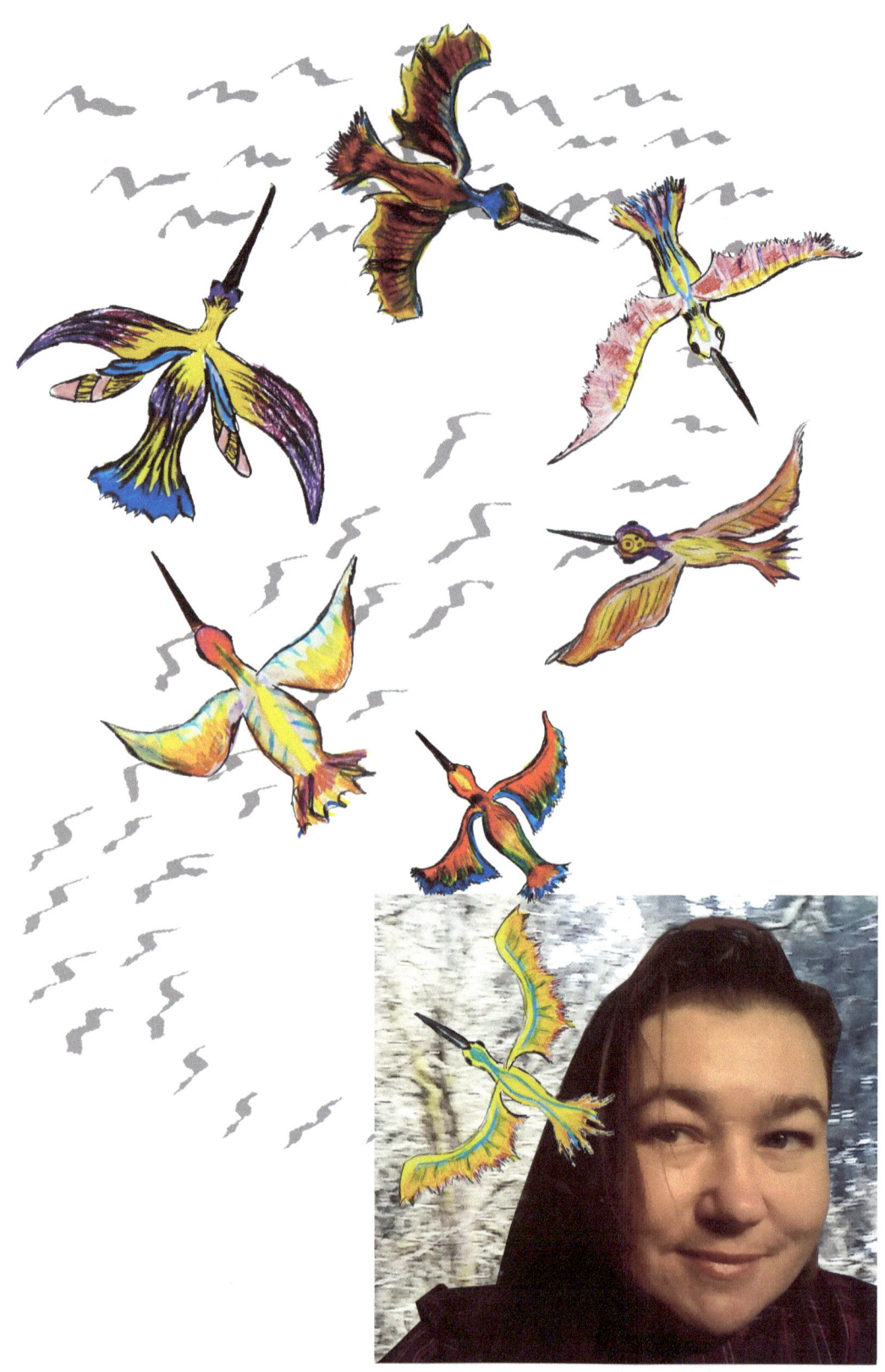

About the Artist:

Janette Bach is an Artist who was raised all over the country but, has become an Oregonian after living in Oregon for 15 years. She has a degree in Fine Art from the California State University of Long Beach and has had a myriad of jobs in the graphic community. She has been the graphic designer for: embroidery and silkscreen shops, print shops, album covers. She has also illustrated a few children's books.

She is an avid fantasy book reader and hiker. This series combines her love of watching birds and the play that can happen in the mind when inspired by the real.

Her Influences for these images are the Audubon Field Guide, Ludwig Bemelmans, Claude Monet, Edouard Manet and Henri Rousseau. A further influence is the prism of the natural world through her mind.

They are sketched, flushed out in acrylics and finished with color pencils. These images were made to share her internal world and inspire all kinds of thoughts.

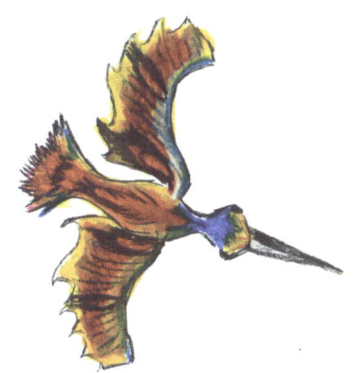

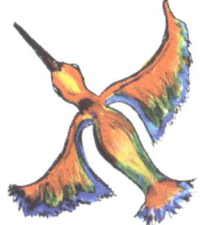

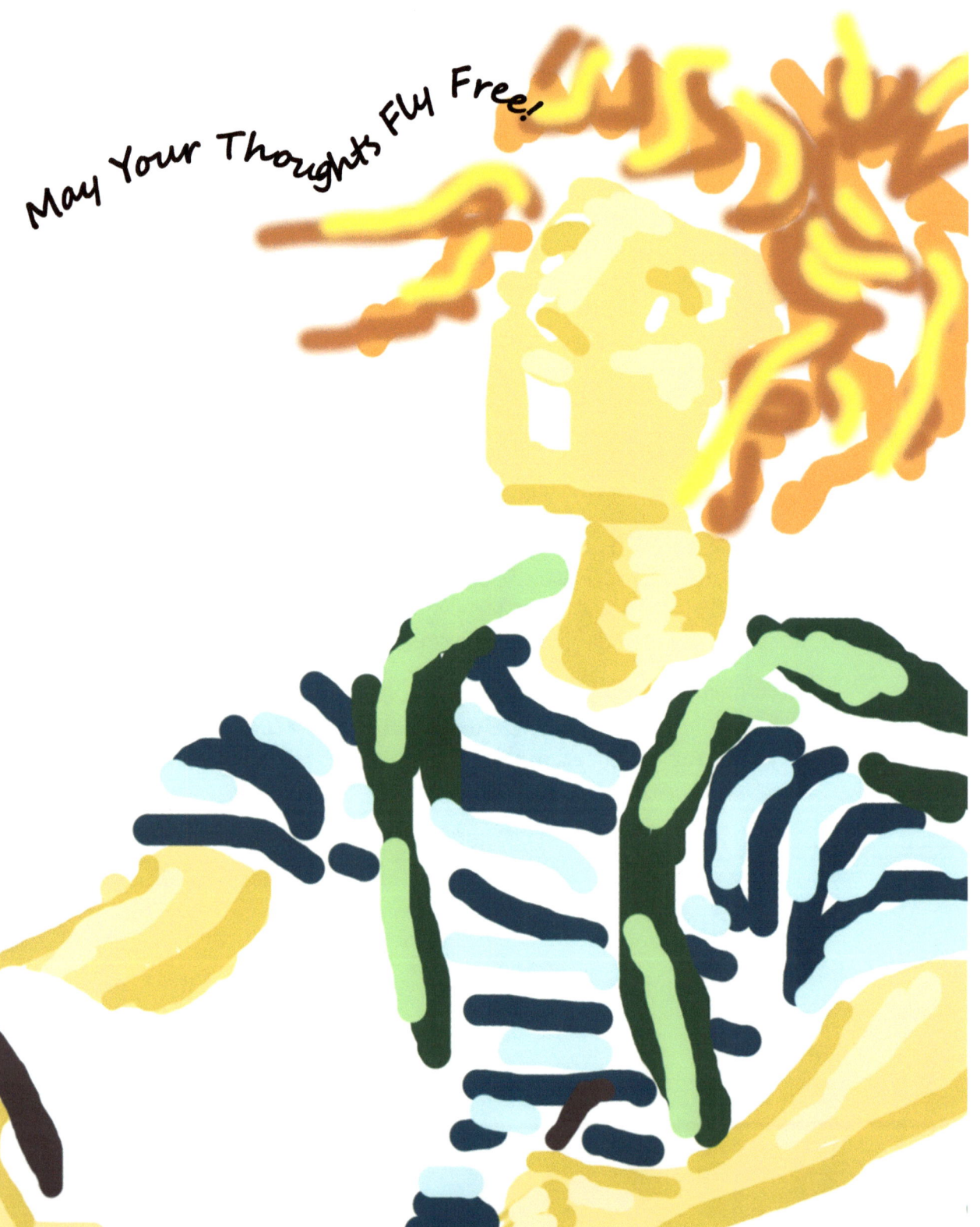